SAN FRA

Published by Gallery Books
A Division of W.H. Smith Publishers Inc.
112 Madison Avenue
New York, New York 10016

Produced by
Brompton Books Corp.
15 Sherwood Place
Greenwich, CT 06830

ISBN 0-8317-7682-X

Printed in Hong Kong

3 4 5 6 7 8 9 10

NCISCO

PHOTOGRAPHY	MARCELLO BERTINETTI ANGELA WHITE BERTINETTI
TEXT	VALERIA MANFERTO DE FABIANIS
DESIGN	CARLO DE FABIANIS

GALLERY BOOKS
An Imprint of W. H. Smith Publishers Inc.
112 Madison Avenue
New York City 10016

To little Diana and Alessandro

Preface

San Francisco is, beyond any doubt, one of the world's most beloved cities. Indeed, in America it is often referred to as 'Everyone's favorite town.' And San Francisco is unique; it is unlike any other city in the world. Life here is more peaceful, more relaxed, more laid back. The city doesn't have the noise or anxiety that is so characteristic of other major urban areas. This is partly because of its history and the events that have caused it to change over the years.

In 1847 San Francisco was nothing more than a small fishing town of some 1000 inhabitants. All of its business activities were focused on the Pacific Ocean and San Francisco Bay. There was no industry and very little agricultural activity in the surrounding area. The discovery of gold at Sutter's Mill and the resultant gold rush in 1848 completely changed the small village. By 1850 the population numbered 35,000. Industries blossomed and agriculture became more and more important to the city's economy. In a few years San Francisco became the main West Coast port in the United States: by 1900 its population had soared to some 340,000, and it was undergoing a corresponding economic and cultural expansion.

Then came the violent earthquake of 18 April 1906 and the fire that raged through the town for three days. The entire business area and a total of 497 blocks in the heart of the city were burned out, resulting in the loss of 452 lives and $350 million worth of damage. During those terrible days, Jack London, the novelist, wrote with deep sorrow: 'San Francisco has disappeared.' But the people of San Francisco overcame their sorrow and pain and courageously and responsibly reacted to that great catastrophe. They started rebuilding almost before the ashes had cooled. The common will to rebuild gave them a sense of unity that still exists in this city.

By 1915, when the city celebrated the opening of the Panama Canal with the Panama Pacific International Exposition, reconstruction was nearly complete. Starting from St Matthew's Peninsula, where the city's urban nucleus lay, the builders worked their way up the surrounding hills. Only a few buildings had survived the earthquake and the fire, and today they stand as silent witnesses of the city's evolution. The outlines of the modern skyscrapers in the center of the city are in sharp contrast with these stately Victorian houses on the hills. Built of wood and painted in every conceivable color, these houses are treasured by San Franciscans, who call them 'Painted Ladies.' This riot of color is only one aspect of the city's charm, but it is an indication of the individualistic nature of San Francisco's people.

Like many other American cities, San Francisco has a rather complicated ethnic mixture, yet these many cultural groups have learned to live together without friction far more successfully than usual. Let's walk along Grant Avenue, where Chinatown begins—that city within a city with its population of some 75,000. The Chinese arrived here during the time of the Gold Rush, and in the beginning faced many problems and troubles. Linked to their past traditions and habits more than any other ethnic group, the Chinese created a part of their native country in San Francisco. Cantonese is the main language spoken in Chinatown, and many of the inhabitants still wear the traditional short damask coats and the shiny black satin trousers similar to the clothing worn in their homeland earlier in this century. Here one can purchase Chinese food and Chinese herbs and Chinese newspapers.

But Chinatown is only one of the many pleasing and picturesque aspects of San Francisco. Walking along Fisherman's Wharf toward Ghirardelli Square is something like observing life in an acting school. Skillfully made-up young people perform magic tricks, mime, sing, dance, juggle, do acrobatics and play musical instruments of all types.

San Francisco is a colorful city, especially at sunset, when the day slowly surrenders to the night, painting the whole city in shades of red. The most overwhelming sight is the Golden Gate Bridge as it changes colors little by little and seems to stand over the entrance to the bay like an ancient cathedral. The city lights come on one after another and on Telegraph Hill, Coit Tower looks like a brittle transparent crystal, while the futuristic pyramid of the Transamerica Building stands out in the center of the city. On Broadway, in the North Beach section, the garish neon signs spotlight the night life attractions that will pulsate until dawn. Day after day, San Francisco changes, but the color remains—the color of the Painted Ladies, of the bay, of the streets full of flower stalls.

The first time I came to San Francisco, I was surprised by the warmth that the city extended to me. While I walked along the streets and mixed with that lively and heterogeneous crowd, I felt as if I had come home. The feeling was not like the dizziness that I experienced when I first arrived in New York, nor the excitement of my first visit to Paris; it was a strange feeling of being familiar with the streets and the people.

I soon learned that San Francisco gets its charm from its people—not from its architecture, its colors, its sunsets, its bright lights, its mild climate. Somehow these people have learned to respect themselves and others. They accept each other as they are and grant others the same freedom that they want for themselves. Extending freedom to others gives rise to a sense of personal freedom that cannot be matched anywhere else in the world.

Valeria Manferto De Fabianis

San Francisco

San Francisco is located in one of the most beautiful areas in California—indeed, in the world. It branches out from Fisherman's Wharf over 42 hills, which have kept their charm and beauty despite urban development.

The city's center is dominated by the 52-story-high Bank of America skyscraper; by the pyramid of the Transamerica Building, whose strange architecture is outlined by the night lights; and by Coit Tower, built in 1934 on top of Telegraph Hill to honor San Francisco's firemen.

Streets here are laid out in a grid pattern, and many of them climb the steep hills at a frightening angle. In the northwestern part of the city is Golden Gate Park, with over a thousand acres of woods and lakes. It was planned by William McLaren who, in 1968, reclaimed a vast area of sand dunes and turned it into a Garden of Eden.

To the north stands the Golden Gate Bridge and The Presidio, which was originally a Spanish army post and contains about 1500 acres of wooded parkland. Now a US Army post, it includes the long, low adobe building—the Officer's Club—that was built by the Spaniards in 1776, making it the oldest building in the city.

The waterfront is in the northeast corner of the city, and a wide street called the Embarcadero runs along the shore. At the north end of the waterfront is Fisherman's Wharf with its dozens of shops and restaurants and its scores of piers where the fishing boats dock.

The mild weather throughout the year helps make life extremely pleasant in San Francisco.

17 Originally a beach situated between Telegraph Hill and Russian Hill, North Beach lies between Columbus Avenue and Broadway. It was here that the first Italian immigrants, mainly from Genoa and Sicily, settled around 1840, having been attracted by the Gold Rush.

19 Market Street is one of the main arteries of San Francisco, extending from the Ferry Building with its clock tower to the Twin Peaks to the south of the city.

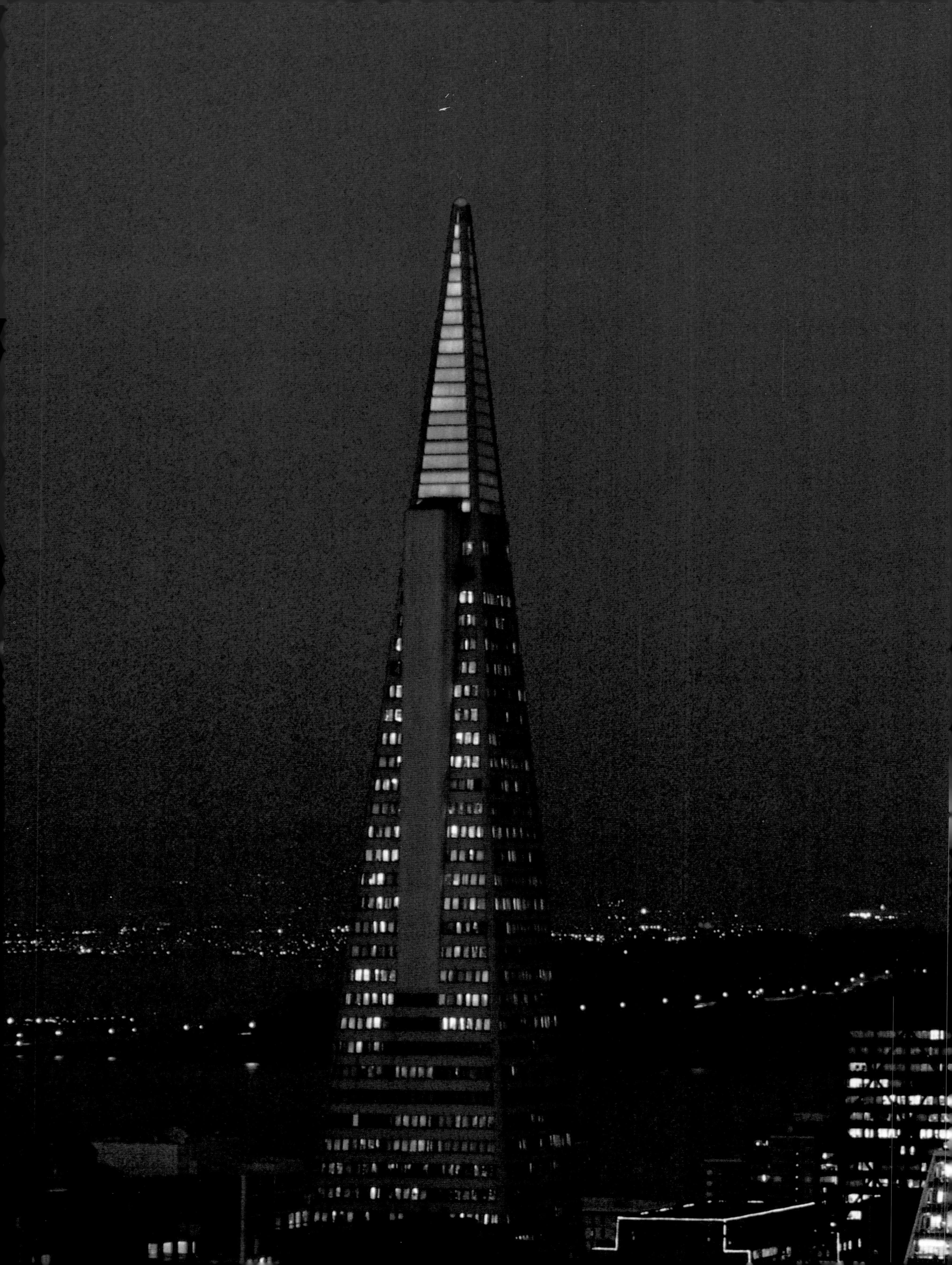

20-22 The San Francisco skyline at night. At left and at right are the city's two highest edifices— the pyramid-like Transamerica Building, and the 52-story world headquarters of the Bank of America.

23 A blue sky graces this view of San Francisco's financial district.

24-25 *San Francisco is surrounded by water on three sides. That is the reason that the city's climate is particularly mild throughout the year, with an average temperature ranging from 40° to 70°F.*

26 *As in many other large American cities, terraces are used in various ways in San Francisco. They may serve as tennis courts, gymnasiums, solariums or even heliports.*

27 *The warm light at sunset softens the outlines of the modern skyscrapers in the center of the city.*

28-29 *The Crown Room of the Fairmont Hotel offers a superb view of the city.*

30 *Lower Pacific Heights and the Marina District looking northwest, with (left to right) the Presidio, the Golden Gate Bridge, and the Marin Headlands in the distance.*

31 An aerial view of San Francisco showing the huge rectangle of Golden Gate Park on the left. Inside the park are gardens, small lakes, museums, sports stadiums, a small zoo and a golf course.

Streets

In 1847 Jasper O'Farrell made the first street plan for the city of San Francisco. Clinging to the tradition of many of America's city maps of that time, he drew a network of parallel streets with other parallel streets intersecting them at right angles—the 'grid system.' Only Columbus Avenue does not conform to this pattern, running crosswise through the city from the water to Jackson Square.

O'Farrell's plan perplexed many people, since it appeared to be unsuitable for the hills of the town. In fact, many streets turned out to be much too steep for the horse—drawn vehicles of the time. In several places the streets rose at an angle of 21 percent, and sidewalks had to be turned into stairways. Indeed, street signs warn motorists to park their cars in gear with the wheels turned toward the curb and the emergency brake on.

Many shops in the city display tee-shirts with 'I've climbed San Francisco's streets' printed on them. Steep though these streets are, the views which can be enjoyed from the hilltops are worth all the physical effort and fatigue involved in the climb.

California Street is one of the city's most famous thoroughfares. The cable cars that travel on this wide avenue maintain a speed of about nine miles per hour. First used in 1878, the cable cars are one of the most important tourist attractions in the city today.

Another famous view is that of Lombard Street, especially when the flower beds along the sharp bends are full of pink hydrangeas. The hidden watersprinklers play with the sun's rays, creating rainbows.

33 Russian Hill was once the site of an old cemetery for Russian sailors; it is now one of San Francisco's most exclusive residential areas.

35 Columbus Avenue passes through most of the city's ethnic neighborhoods.

36-37 No one can deny that Lombard Street is one of the most famous and unusual streets of San Francisco. Situated on Russian Hill, it starts from High Street and goes down to Leavenworth, winding through ten incredibly sharp turns.

38-39 Rescue workers pull up a car which was perched over a collapsed section of the bi-level Oakland Bay Bridge after a severe earthquake rocked the city in October 1989.

40-41 The Bay Bridge was soon repaired and functioning as usual. Although the city's structures are built to withstand earthquakes, some damage is inevitable in a major quake, and municipal agencies are in constant readiness for such emergencies.

42 Columbus Avenue (at left in photo) is the main thoroughfare in the popular North Beach neighborhood. At right, Coit Tower perches on Telegraph Hill. Alcatraz Island can be seen in San Francisco Bay, and the hills of the Marin Headlands are in the background.

43 California Street, where it intersects with Montgomery Street, is the financial center of San Francisco—the 'Wall Street' of the West Coast.

44 San Francisco is the only city in the world with a fully operating system of cable cars.

45 Some of the city's original cable cars have been bought by private operators and now run on diesel engines. They are used for guided tours and parades, such as the annual St. Patrick's Day Parade.

People

It is always interesting to observe a city in the early morning, when life regains its usual rhythm after a night's rest. In San Francisco, the morning awakening seems to take place gradually. First the workers in the financial district arrive in order to be at work when the stock exchanges open in New York City, which is three hours ahead of San Francisco time.

Then the people come down the hills to the center of the city to open their offices, shops, banks and government agencies. Little by little the streets become more crowded, and the cable cars and other traffic contribute to the liveliness. Peddlars' stalls along Fisherman's Wharf and flower stalls all over the city begin to open. Children and the elderly come to Union Square to offer crumbs of bread, pieces of biscuit or handfuls of seed to the pigeons. There is activity even on the terraces of the highest buildings—there people play tennis, exercise, garden or hang out their washing.

On holidays, San Franciscans crowd their beautiful parks. Golden Gate Park is literally overrun, from the fuschia garden to the music garden where concerts and dances are held. Dozens of brightly colored sails can be seen in San Francisco Bay and passing under the arcades of the Golden Gate Bridge.

The people of San Francisco have a cheerful and warm-hearted nature, and they deeply love their city—constantly defending its traditions against creeping urbanization. For example, a few years ago it was proposed to substitute more modern and efficient means of transportation for the cable cars. This was overwhelmingly rejected by the people.

47 The Chinese make up the main ethnic group in San Francisco.

49 Spontaneity and a joy of living are the main characteristics of the people of San Francisco. It seems that everywhere in the streets, squares or parks one finds somebody willing to put on an extemporaneous performance.

50 San Francisco is considered one of the most elegant and refined cities in the United States, as this woman's appearance can testify.

51 San Franciscans say that the mild weather is good for the soul and the spirit, and that is why girls have such a fresh and charming look.

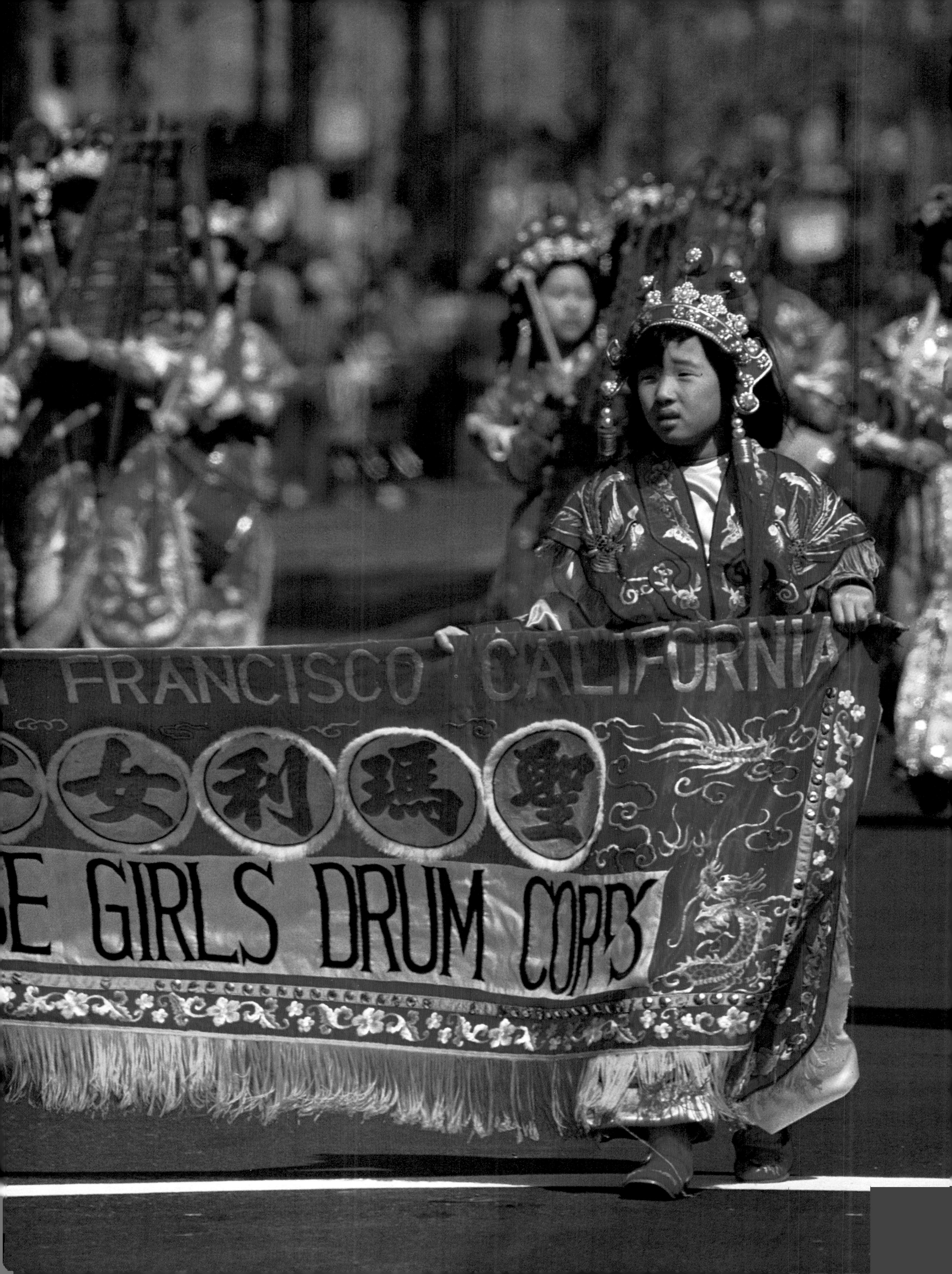
FRANCISCO CALIFORNIA
女利瑪聖
GIRLS DRUM

52-53 Golden Gate Park was planned to be used by the people.

54-55 In San Francisco respect for old habits and traditions of the various ethnic groups is almost a holy thing.

56-57 The whole city of San Francisco could be considered a living theater. It seems that everywhere one can run into musicians, jugglers or actors.

58-59 San Francisco Bay on a sunny day is gorgeous.

60 Enthusiasm is one of the traits of a true San Francisco resident, and the children are, as everywhere, the living example of this joyful trait.

61 The urge to relax is respected everywhere in San Francisco. Even on noisy holidays in the parks, it is always possible to withdraw just to rest a bit or to read without being interrupted.

62 Flowers on windowsills, on street-corner, stands, in the flower beds adorning sky-scrapers or in the hands of a beautiful woman are the symbol of the everlasting springtime of San Francisco.

63 The city is colored green on St Patrick's Day. Green balloons adorn Union Square, green waters come from fountains, shamrocks are displayed in store windows,˙ and the people dress to echo the theme.

64 San Francisco's police watch over the city to ensure order and respect for the law.

65 All San Franciscans can express their beliefs, and homosexuality is respected in those who choose it.

66 San Francisco cares about its children. In Golden Gate Park there is a large area totally reserved for children, where a children's zoo can be found.

67 San Francisco is a city for all races.

68 Rain does not interrupt the rhythm of the city.

69 Rain is not a source of gloom here. On the contrary, the many-colored umbrellas dress the city in a new and special cheerfulness.

Painted Ladies

Some 48,000 Victorian houses were built in San Francisco between 1850 and 1915. Many of them burned down during the fire of 1906, but those that escaped destruction and those that were built subsequently are the pride of San Francisco.

There was a time when their many-colored facades showed the wear and tear of wind, rain and time. Their decorations were falling down and their colors were fading. The Painted Ladies were losing their charm and were aging away. Then the people of San Francisco once again defended their traditions. The city itself promoted a competition to refurbish the Painted Ladies, and the result was an incredible enthusiasm on the part of the homeowners.

The houses were repaired and replastered exactly as they had been before, and all facades were repainted in their original bright colors. Broken panes were replaced with colorful stained glass windows, the balconies were decorated with flowers in pots, the gardens were weeded and reseeded. After the judges had reached a decision, the winner received a free vacation and a pair of jogging shoes.

Each of these houses has a personality of its own, but most of them have several things in common—latticed windows, entrances with thin columns, inlays, geometric or floral decorations, grand staircases and oddly shaped roofs. These houses are not of a single architectural type, but rather range from Queen Anne Revival to Gothic. They reflect the tastes of middle-class San Franciscans who got rich during the Gold Rush—that period of 'the last frontier.'

71 *Respect for historical monuments is felt in a special way in San Francisco. There are old restored houses to be found in almost every section of the city.*

73 *Owners of the old Victorian houses feel extremely proud of having contributed to the city's historical tradition by their restoration efforts.*

74 *The Painted Ladies were built in four architectural styles: the Queen Anne, an English style of about 1860; the Italianate, inspired by the Italian Renaissance; the Georgian, which prevailed in England between 1702 and 1830; and the Stick, created by the English architect Sir Charles Locke Eastlake.*

75 *The front yards of the Victorian houses lend elegance to the entrances adorned with short stairs and thin columns.*

76-77 *These houses, built in the Queen Anne style, are situated in Alamo Square and were built by Matthew Kavanaugh in 1894 and 1895. They are among the most famous in San Francisco.*

78-79 *This Stick style house, situated on Washington Street, dates back to 1885. The restoration work began in 1960.*

The Golden Gate Bridge

The beginning of the construction of the Golden Gate Bridge dates back to 1930—an important historical period in the United States. It was the era of the Great Depression, the New Deal and the effort to achieve an economic recovery after the Wall Street Crash of 1929. The American people had to use all their courage and resources to face and overcome hardships and privations.

It was also an era of risky ventures, and the construction of the Golden Gate Bridge was a part of this, along with such other monumental tasks as the building of Rockefeller Center in New York City. These projects still stand as reminders of the indomitable spirit of the American people and of their will to overcome adversity.

The bridge was proposed by Joseph Strauss who, before he could begin construction, had to overcome not only the skepticism of the people, but their outright opposition. It was, without doubt, a big venture. The bridge frame was revolutionary. Work began on 5 February 1933, and construction was completed four years later. On 7 May 1937 the bridge was opened by President Franklin Delano Roosevelt.

Ever since then, the Golden Gate Bridge has been the most famous symbol of San Francisco; it has never lost its capacity to inspire awe and amazement.

81 The Golden Gate Bridge—a unique construction.

83 The Golden Gate Bridge supports six lanes of traffic as well as two pedestrian lanes.

84-85 The builders of the bridge faced a lot of problems, such as the water's swift current and the fierceness of the wind. The bridge was constructed to withstand a windstorm of 100 mph.

86-87 The Golden Gate Bridge stands out from the backdrop formed by the lights of San Francisco.

88 The Golden Gate Bridge can take a lot of strain. The height of the road surface can vary by more than seven feet, depending on the temperature and the traffic.

89 The Golden Gate Bridge holds two un-usual records—the fewest number of workers killed while it was under construction, and the highest number of suicides.

90 The distance between the two 740-foot-high towers of the bridge measures over 4000 feet.

91 Two days of celebration highlighted the opening of the Golden Gate Bridge. More than 200,000 people crossed the bridge on foot on the first day.

92 The shifting light constantly changes the appearance of the bridge.

93 At night, the head and tail lights of the automobiles on the bridge look like a luminous waterfall.

Viewpoints

During the warmest months, San Francisco turns into a great garden. On many street corners, flower stalls display beautiful bunches of blooms. Everywhere there is a riot of colors and scents—at the feet of the skyscrapers, in front of the houses, on the balconies and on the hills.

In the shopping sections the display windows are decorated in such a graceful and tasteful manner that sometimes the reflected lights seems to make the mannequins come alive.

In North Beach—the Italian quarter—the bars are crowded, while winking neon lights invite customers to taste a really good cappuccino in the many restaurants.

In the residential area near Golden Gate Park, an absolute stillness reigns—children play in the streets from which the traffic has disappeared while mounted policemen discreetly patrol the avenues.

Open windows let the sunshine into the houses. Like hedges and fences, heavy drapes are rare in San Francisco, where the people do not feel as threatened by proximity as they do in most other cities.

95 San Franciscans are rightfully proud of the city's plentiful historic architecture, and make sure that it is carefully preserved.

97 A beautiful view of one of the modern skyscrapers in San Francisco.

98 The Oakland Bay Bridge, opened in 1936, links San Francisco to Oakland across the bay.

99 A view of the Crocker Center Gallery's glass dome.

100-101 The Crocker Center Gallery has three floors with 60 elegant shops and two restaurants. During the day, the sun lights up the hall, filtering through the glass dome that overhangs the whole gallery.

102-103 The Italian section in North Beach is famous for its restaurants, bakeries and special food shops. Everywhere there is the smell of Italian cooking and the strong fragrance of espresso coffee.

104-105 San Francisco's police are efficient in their patrolling of the streets and maintaining order.

106 Ferry tours to Alcatraz Island are a popular attraction for visitors.

107 A tour bus with an advertisement for
Ghirardelli Square—a complex of stores,
restaurants and theaters at the end of
Fisherman's Wharf.

108 *The lobby of the Fairmont Hotel on Nob Hill.*

109 *The Neiman Marcus department store in Union Square.*

Inside the windows: OPEN EVERY DAY · SAN FRANCISCO FLORAL SERVICE · BALLOONS DELIVERED

110 The brightness of shop windows reflects the joyful nature of the people of San Francisco.

111 An elegant shop on Nob Hill. 'Nob' is a distortion of the word 'Nabob,' an old-fashioned epithet for a millionaire.

Lights

Light is an essential feature of San Francisco's charm. Since it is always changing, it produces an endless metamorphosis of shapes and colors. At dawn, the city can be wrapped in a low mist that hides all but the tops of the highest skyscrapers. Then, during the day, the sun and the clouds can change the city from what appears to be a warm and bright Mediterranean village into a gray Nordic town.

The sun diversifies the colors of the houses, while the clouds soften them. At sunset the beauty of San Francisco reaches its height. A big red sun colors the Golden Gate Bridge arcades before plunging into the Pacific. Behind the bridge the city seems to turn pink, while the hills in the distance appear to fade away in a thin layer of haze.

At sunset time, things can take on a surrealistic view. A thin layer of clouds hides San Francisco Bay. Only the Golden Gate Bridge towers, which seem to be floating in empty space, stand against the blue sky.

But it is at night that one can fully enjoy the true beauty of San Francisco, when it quivers with multicolored lights.

113 *Neon signs on Broadway reflect on the hood of a car during a shower.*

115 *Lights on the Golden Gate Bridge produce an eerie glow as the city is enveloped in fog.*

116-117 Like all big cities, San Francisco takes on a new look at night.

118-119 The warm sunset softens the stern lines of the skyscrapers.

120 A view of Chinatown at night.

121 Evening falls behind a San Francisco skyscraper.

122 Coit Tower at night. The tower was built on Telegraph Hill in 1933 in memory of the city's firemen and was named after Lillie Hitchcock Coit, who was such a fan of the fire department that she was made an honorary volunteer fireman.

123 Russian Hill is one of the most elegant sections of San Francisco.

124-125 The red metallic color of the Golden Gate Bridge reflecting the sunset light.

126 The waves that break in the Golden Gate create ideal conditions for surfing.